世代與階級的雙重不平等

The Double Inequality of Generation and Class

徐萍 Ping Xu

Preface 前言

我們所處的時代，充滿一種隱形卻普遍的焦慮。
上一代人深信「努力考試、拿到文憑，就能出人頭地」，
但這個公式在今日已經失效。分數不再是學習的象徵，
而成了焦慮的起點；文憑不再是能力的證明，
而淪為權力的門票。當幻象破滅，
年輕人卻被迫承受失落與壓力。

We live in an era haunted by a silent yet pervasive anxiety. The older generation firmly believed that “hard work, good test scores, and a diploma” guaranteed success. That formula has collapsed. Scores have become the source of anxiety rather than symbols of learning; diplomas have turned from evidence of ability into tickets of privilege. When the illusion shatters, it is the young who are left to bear the weight of disappointment.

這本書要談的，正是這種幻象與現實之間的落差。
我稱之為「世代不正義」。它不只是台灣的問題，
也不只是中國的現象，而是一個跨國的文明挑戰。
年輕人陷入低薪、債務、住房困境，甚至不敢生育；
長輩則依舊以舊公式要求後代。這種撕裂不只在家庭之間，
也在整個社會的制度深處。

This book is about that gap between illusion and reality—what I call generational injustice. It is not only Taiwan’s issue, nor solely China’s phenomenon, but a civilizational challenge crossing borders. Young people are trapped in low wages, debt, and unaffordable housing, often too fearful to start families. Elders still impose outdated formulas, deepening the rift not only between generations but within the very core of our institutions.

我要提醒讀者：世代不正義並不是偶然，
而是制度設計的結果。既然是人為的，就能被重新設計。
這本書不是要提供簡單的答案，而是要打開一扇視窗，
讓我們看見：問題如何形成、在哪裡加劇、
為什麼拖延至今、又該如何走向一份新的文明契約。

I want to remind the reader: generational injustice is not accidental. It is the outcome of system design. And because it is man-made, it can be redesigned. This book does not promise easy answers. Instead, it seeks to open a window—showing how the problem took shape, where it intensifies, why it has persisted, and how we might move toward a new civilizational contract.

第一章：
分數、文憑與制度的陷阱

Chapter One:
The Trap of Scores, Diplomas, and Systems

第一節：分數怪物的誕生
Section 1: The Birth of the Score Monster

在教室裡，分數原本只是檢視學習成果的工具，卻逐漸演變為評價一個人價值的唯一標準。當「幾分」比「學到什麼」更重要時，學生被迫投入無止境的考試循環。
父母、老師、媒體共同建構出一種幻象：
考不好就等於沒有未來。於是，「分數怪物」誕生了，
它吞噬童年的好奇心，也壓抑了學習的樂趣。

In the classroom, scores were originally meant to be a tool for assessing learning. Yet over time, they became the sole measure of worth. When "how many points you scored" mattered more than "what you actually learned," students were pushed into an endless cycle of exams. Parents, teachers, and media reinforced this illusion, making children believe that a low score meant a failed future. Thus, the "Score Monster" was born—devouring curiosity and suffocating the joy of learning.

第二節：文憑蠢貨的養成
Section 2: The Making of the Diploma Fool

當「分數怪物」長大，它最終結出另一種產物——「文憑蠢貨」。名校的文憑成為進入權力與資源的門票。教育不再是知識與思考的證明，而只是象徵權威的入場券。這些靠著分數堆疊而來的菁英，往往誤以為自己擁有智慧，卻缺乏整合、判斷與創新的能力。他們把治理當作考試，把政策視為標準答案，卻無法處理人性與社會的複雜性。於是，教育製造出一批「文憑蠢貨」，占據決策位置，卻無力解決真實問題。

When the “Score Monster” grows up, it produces another creature—the “Diploma Fool.” Prestigious diplomas become tickets to power and resources. Education is no longer proof of wisdom but merely an entry pass to authority. Those who climbed up by piling scores mistake credentials for competence, yet lack integration, judgment, and creativity. They govern as if answering an exam, with no ability to deal with human complexity. Thus, education manufactures “Diploma Fools”—decision-makers incapable of solving real problems.

第三節：教育如何墮落為陷阱
Section 3: How Education Became a Trap

教育原本應該是希望的管道，讓人拓展視野、培養能力、實現潛能。然而，在分數與文憑的雙重挾制下，它墮落為焦慮的陷阱。學生學習，不再是為了探索世界，而是為了避免落後。學校不再是思想與人格的養成場域，而是大量製造文憑的工廠。當制度幻象崩解，人們才驚覺：自己耗費十幾二十年的青春，只是被馴化成體制裡的齒輪。

Education was supposed to be a channel of hope—expanding horizons, nurturing abilities, and realizing potential. Yet under the dual domination of scores and diplomas, it has degenerated into a trap of anxiety. Students learn not to explore the world but to avoid falling behind. Schools no longer shape minds and character, but mass-produce diplomas. When the illusion collapses, people realize they spent their youth being tamed into cogs of the system.

第四節：制度幻象的崩解與世代不正義的種子
Section 4: The Collapse of Illusions and the Seeds of Injustice

分數與文憑構築的幻象，不僅壓迫個人，也為世代不正義埋下伏筆。上一代深信「努力考試就能成功」，並把這種公式強加在下一代身上。然而，當社會流動停滯、文憑失去保障時，青年卻承受雙倍壓力：既要證明自己，又要面對幻象崩潰的失落。這正是分數怪物與文憑蠢貨最殘酷的遺產——它們不僅毀掉教育，也撕裂了世代。

The illusion built on scores and diplomas not only crushes individuals but also lays the foundation for generational injustice. The older generation believed in the formula "hard work plus exams equals success" and imposed it on the young. Yet as mobility froze and diplomas lost value, the youth bore a double burden: proving themselves while enduring the collapse of illusions. This is the cruelest legacy of the Score Monster and the Diploma Fool—they destroy education and fracture generations.

分數與文憑的陷阱揭示了幻象如何崩潰成不正義。
教育本應是希望的階梯，卻變成焦慮的牢籠。
這正是世代不正義的起點。在下一章，我們將走進台灣，
看見22K世代、買不起的房、
以及年金壓力如何勾勒出最鮮明的世代困境。

The trap of scores and diplomas shows us how illusions collapse into injustice. What was meant to be a ladder of hope became a cage of anxiety. This is the beginning of generational injustice. In the next chapter, we turn to Taiwan, where the struggles of the 22K generation, unaffordable housing, and pension burdens reveal the sharpest outlines of this injustice.

Chapter Two:
Generational Injustice in Taiwan

第二章：台灣的世代不正義

第一節：22K低薪世代的困境
Section 1: The Trap of the 22K Generation

在台灣，「22K」幾乎成了整整一代人的符號。
2008年金融危機後，政府推動「青年就業方案」，
給予企業補助，
讓大學畢業生以新台幣22,000元的起薪進入職場。
原本只是短期的政策，卻逐漸固化成整個世代的薪資標籤。
十幾年過去，物價上升、房價飆漲，但薪水卻依舊停滯不前。年輕人發現，自己不是在職場上逐步成長，
而是被困在一個無形的低薪陷阱裡。

In Taiwan, “22K” has become a symbol of an entire generation. After the 2008 financial crisis, the government introduced a “youth employment program,” subsidizing companies to hire college graduates at a starting salary of NT$22,000. What was meant to be a temporary policy solidified into a generational wage ceiling. More than a decade later, while prices and housing costs soared, wages stagnated. Young people discovered they were not climbing the career ladder but trapped in an invisible cage of low pay.

第二節：買不起的家，斷裂的未來
Section 2: The Unaffordable Home and the Broken Future

在父母那一代，房子是努力存錢即可達成的夢想；
在子女這一代，房子卻成為遙不可及的奢望。
台灣的房價所得比早已飆破全球平均，
青年即使工作十年，也難以湊到頭期款。
父母輩常以「我們當年也是咬牙買下來的」來回應，
卻忽略了物價、薪資與資產累積環境的徹底不同。
房子不只是居住空間，更是社會流動的象徵。
當年輕人連安身之所都無法企及，未來的希望自然斷裂。

For the parent generation, owning a home was a dream achievable through hard work and saving. For today's youth, it has become a distant luxury. Taiwan's house price-to-income ratio has long exceeded global averages, making it nearly impossible for young workers to save enough for a down payment, even after ten years of work. Parents often respond with, "We also struggled to buy a house back then," but they overlook the radically different context of wages, prices, and asset accumulation. Housing is not just shelter—it is a symbol of social mobility. When young people cannot even secure a place to live, the promise of the future fractures.

第三節：少子化與年金壓力
Section 3: Declining Birthrates and Pension Burdens

台灣的少子化並非只是「不想生」，而是「不敢生」。
高房價、低薪資與不穩定的工作環境，讓年輕人感到撫養下一代是一種風險。與此同時，台灣的年金制度又成為另一層枷鎖。老一輩的退休保障，靠的是後輩勞工的繳款。然而當勞動人口逐年減少，負擔卻愈來愈重。青年一方面被期待成家立業，一方面又必須背負沉重的養老責任。這種「兩頭燒」的結構矛盾，正是世代不正義的具體體現。

Taiwan's declining birthrate is not merely about "not wanting children" but "not daring to have them." High housing costs, low wages, and unstable jobs make raising the next generation feel like a financial risk. At the same time, Taiwan's pension system imposes another burden: retirees rely on contributions from younger workers. As the workforce shrinks, the weight on youth grows heavier. They are expected to start families while also funding an aging population. This "double bind" structure is a direct manifestation of generational injustice.

第四節：制度陷阱——政策的短視與扭曲
Section 4: Structural Traps — Policy Myopia and Distortion

台灣的政策設計往往「頭痛醫頭、腳痛醫腳」。22K方案沒有消失，卻成了低薪合理化的藉口；青年租金補助推出，卻又推升了租屋市場的價格；年金改革遲遲不敢觸動既得利益，卻加深了世代對立。這些政策並非真正解決問題，而是以短視的補丁措施延續困境。制度陷阱不只困住年輕人，也讓整個社會走向惡性循環。

Taiwanese policymaking often follows the logic of "treating symptoms, not causes." The 22K program lingered and became a justification for wage stagnation; rent subsidies were introduced but ended up inflating rental prices; pension reform avoided confronting vested interests, deepening generational divides. Such policies do not solve problems but perpetuate them through short-sighted patches. These structural traps ensnare not only the youth but the entire society in a vicious cycle.

第五節：文化盲點——長輩的誤解與壓力
Section 5: Cultural Blind Spots – The Misunderstandings and Pressure from Elders

台灣社會有一種深植的盲點：上一代相信努力必有收穫，
卻無法理解結構性環境已經翻轉。
當年輕人表達無力感時，常被批評為「草莓族」「不夠努力」。
這種世代間的誤解，不僅加重了青年的焦慮，
也掩蓋了制度的責任。父母的「過來人經驗」
反而成了壓力來源，迫使青年背負不可能實現的期待。

A deeply rooted blind spot in Taiwanese society is the belief of the older generation that hard work always pays off. They fail to see that structural conditions have fundamentally changed. When young people voice their struggles, they are often dismissed as the “strawberry generation” or accused of not working hard enough. Such generational misunderstandings not only exacerbate anxiety but also mask systemic responsibility. Parents’ “been there, done that” experiences turn into sources of pressure, forcing youth to shoulder expectations that are no longer realistic.

第六節：心理後果——焦慮、倦怠與幻滅
Section 6: Psychological Consequences – Anxiety, Burnout, and Disillusionment

長期處於低薪、買不起房、少子化與年金壓力的結構中，青年世代普遍陷入焦慮與倦怠。有人選擇「躺平」，有人透過移民尋找出口，有人則陷入抑鬱與倦怠之中。這不僅是個人情緒問題，而是制度所造成的集體心理後果。當一個世代對未來失去信任，社會也就失去了前進的動能。

Caught in the structural web of low wages, unaffordable housing, declining birthrates, and pension burdens, Taiwan's youth suffer widespread anxiety and burnout. Some choose to "lie flat," others seek escape through emigration, while many fall into depression and exhaustion. This is not merely an individual emotional issue but a collective psychological consequence of systemic failure. When a generation loses faith in the future, society loses its driving force.

台灣的世代不正義，不只是經濟困境，更是制度陷阱、
文化盲點與心理後果交織的結果。22K低薪世代、買不起的房、
少子化與年金壓力，不僅壓縮了青年的生活，
也撕裂了世代間的信任。這些現象並非台灣獨有，
而是全球世代危機的一部分。
下一章，我們將把目光轉向中國。那裡的「內卷」「學歷貶值」
「六個錢包」「421家庭」與「躺平」，
同樣揭示了另一種世代不正義的面貌，
並與台灣形成鮮明的對照。

Taiwan's generational injustice is not merely about economic hardship but the entanglement of structural traps, cultural blind spots, and psychological consequences. The 22K low-wage generation, the unaffordable housing crisis, declining birthrates, and pension burdens not only squeeze the lives of the young but also erode trust between generations. These issues are not unique to Taiwan—they are part of a broader global generational crisis.
In the next chapter, we will turn to China. There, "involution," "credential inflation," "six wallets," the "421 family structure," and the phenomenon of "lying flat" reveal another face of generational injustice—one that sharply contrasts with Taiwan while echoing similar struggles.

第三章：
中國的世代不正義

Chapter 3:
Generational Injustice in China

第一節 內卷與學歷貶值
Section 1: Involution and the Devaluation of Degrees

在中國，「內卷」成了年輕世代最精準的寫照。從小學、初中到大學，學生投入大量時間金錢參加補習、考試，卻發現即便拿到大學文憑，也無法換來穩定工作。學歷通膨導致大學生畢業即失業，研究所、博士人數暴增，卻依然擠不進有限的好職位。當努力不再帶來上升通道，年輕人只能陷入無止境的競爭與焦慮，這就是「內卷」的真實含義。

In China, the term "involution" has become the most precise description of the younger generation. From primary school through university, students invest enormous time and money in tutoring and exams, only to find that even a college degree no longer guarantees stable employment. With diploma inflation, graduates face unemployment, while soaring numbers of master's and PhD holders still struggle to secure limited positions. When effort no longer produces upward mobility, young people become trapped in endless competition and anxiety—this is the true meaning of "involution."

第二節 六個錢包與住房絕望
Section 2: The “Six Wallets” and the Despair of Housing

在中國的一線城市，買房已成為青年與家庭的共同噩夢。
房價高到必須動員父母與祖父母的積蓄，
形成所謂「六個錢包」才能湊齊首付。
這不僅讓青年失去獨立生活的可能，也加劇了代際矛盾：
上一代視買房為「責任」，而年輕人則視之為「枷鎖」。
當住房被徹底金融化，青年世代只能背負
沉重貸款進入人生，或乾脆放棄擁有房子的夢想。

In China’s first-tier cities, buying a home has become a nightmare shared by both youth and their families. Prices are so high that parents and grandparents must pool their savings—the so-called “six wallets”—just to afford a down payment. This strips young people of independence and heightens intergenerational tension: the older generation sees homeownership as a duty, while the young see it as a shackle. With housing fully financialized, the younger generation is left either burdened with crushing mortgages or forced to abandon the dream of ever owning a home.

第三節 421家庭結構的重擔
Section 3: The 4-2-1 Family Structure and Its Crushing Burden

一胎化政策留下了「421家庭結構」:
四位老人、一對夫妻、一個孩子。
這意味著青年世代不僅要撫養子女，
還要同時承擔四位長輩的養老與醫療開支。
當社會保障不足、醫療資源昂貴，
這種家庭結構讓年輕人幾乎無法喘息。
他們既是經濟支柱，也是情感支柱，
卻常常在壓力下選擇不婚不育，
進一步加劇少子化與人口危機。

China’s one-child policy created the “4-2-1 family structure”: four grandparents, two parents, and one child. This leaves the younger generation not only responsible for raising children but also supporting four elderly relatives’ retirement and healthcare. With inadequate social security and costly medical services, this structure leaves young people with little room to breathe. They are expected to be both the financial and emotional backbone, yet under such pressure many choose not to marry or have children, further accelerating demographic decline.

第四節 躺平與隱性抗爭
Section 4: Lying Flat and the Politics of Silent Resistance

當努力無法換來希望，年輕人開始用「躺平」來表達抗議。
這不是懶惰，而是一種被動的抵抗：拒絕過度工作、
拒絕內卷競爭、拒絕被當作犧牲品。網路上流行的
「擺爛」與「躺平主義」，正是青年面對制度
不正義時的心理防衛機制。
當制度不給出出路，青年便用沉默的方式退出遊戲，
這種隱性的抗爭本身，就是對世代不義最尖銳的控訴。

When hard work no longer brings hope, young people turn to “lying flat” as a form of protest. This is not laziness but passive resistance: rejecting overwork, rejecting involution, rejecting being treated as expendable. Online trends like “let it rot” and the “lying flat movement” reflect a psychological defense against systemic injustice. When institutions provide no exit, the young respond by quietly withdrawing from the game—a silent form of resistance that stands as the sharpest indictment of generational injustice.

中國的世代不正義，呈現的是「高速發展之後的代價」：
教育內卷、住房金融化、養老重擔與躺平抗爭。
這些現象看似彼此獨立，實際上卻構成一個完整的惡性循環——青年被困在無休止的競爭裡，被迫承擔家庭與社會的成本，最後只能以退出回應幻象的崩解。與台灣相比，中國的問題規模更龐大，壓力更集中，但結論卻相同：當一個世代普遍失去希望，文明就站在臨界點。
下一章，我們將把視野推向全球，觀察日本的失落世代、歐美的千禧困境，以及氣候危機如何放大代際的不平等。

Generational injustice in China reveals "the cost of rapid development": educational involution, housing financialization, eldercare burdens, and the resistance of lying flat. These phenomena may appear separate, but together they form a vicious cycle—youth trapped in endless competition, forced to shoulder family and social costs, and ultimately responding to collapsing illusions by opting out. Compared with Taiwan, China's issues are larger in scale and sharper in intensity, but the conclusion is the same: when an entire generation loses hope, civilization stands at a tipping point. In the next chapter, we broaden our lens to the global stage, exploring Japan's lost generation, the millennial struggles in the West, and how the climate crisis amplifies intergenerational inequality.

第四章：
全球世代不正義的對照

Chapter Four:
Global Parallels of Generational Injustice

第一節：日本的失落世代
Section 1: Japan's Lost Generation

日本的「失落世代」誕生於泡沫經濟破滅之後。
大量青年畢業即遭遇「就業冰河期」，終生僅能從事派遣工、
短期合約等非典型工作。對許多人來說，
職涯的第一步就已被卡死，沒有累積年資、沒有升遷機會、
沒有未來保障。這不僅是個人悲劇，更成為國家
人口結構與經濟發展的長期負擔。
失落世代在中年之後，常面臨「既無積蓄又無年金」
的窘境，直接揭示了體制在危機中對青年的拋棄。

Japan's "Lost Generation" was born in the aftermath of the economic bubble's collapse. Countless young people graduated straight into an "employment ice age," spending their lives in dispatch work or short-term contracts. For many, their first step in the labor market was already blocked—no seniority to accumulate, no opportunities for promotion, no future security. This was not only an individual tragedy but a structural burden on demographics and the economy. Entering middle age, many of the Lost Generation face the bleak reality of "no savings, no pension," exposing how the system abandoned its youth during crisis.

第二節：歐美千禧世代的困境
Section 2: The Struggles of Western Millennials

歐美的千禧世代成長於金融化與全球化的時代。他們被鼓勵借貸上大學，卻畢業即陷入龐大的學貸負擔；他們經歷過2008年金融海嘯，剛踏入職場就面對失業與不穩定；他們在疫情之後，進一步感受到房價與生活成本的急速上漲。於是，一整個世代在「學貸未清、薪資停滯、房價高漲」的三重壓力下前行。雖然手握文憑，卻沒有階級流動的保障；雖然身處先進國家，卻依然感到未來比過去更黯淡。

The millennial generation in Europe and America came of age during financialization and globalization. They were encouraged to borrow heavily for college, only to graduate with crushing debt. They entered the labor market amid the 2008 financial crisis, facing unemployment and instability from the start. After the pandemic, they confronted soaring housing prices and living costs. Thus, an entire generation moves forward under the triple pressure of “student debt, stagnant wages, rising housing costs.” They hold diplomas without mobility, live in advanced nations yet feel their futures are dimmer than their pasts.

第三節：租不起的一代
Section 3: The Generation That Can't Afford Rent

在全球許多城市，房價與租金高漲，造就了「租不起的一代」。倫敦、紐約、巴黎、雪梨、東京，青年不僅無法購屋，連租屋也成為沈重負擔。他們往往必須與數名室友合租狹小空間，或是遠距通勤數小時，只為了勉強維持生活。當「安身立命」的基礎條件消失，青年不再期待「向上流動」，反而轉向「如何生存」。這種轉變不僅影響生活型態，也逐漸侵蝕社會的穩定與信任。

In many global cities, skyrocketing housing prices and rents have created the "generation that can't afford rent." From London and New York to Paris, Sydney, and Tokyo, young people cannot buy homes and struggle even to rent. They often share cramped spaces with multiple roommates or endure multi-hour commutes from distant suburbs, just to scrape by. When the basic condition of "having a place to live" disappears, youth shift from aspiring to "upward mobility" to focusing solely on "basic survival." This shift alters lifestyles and gradually erodes social stability and trust.

第四節：氣候變遷與代際倫理危機
Section 4: Climate Change and the Ethics of Generations

除了經濟與住房，氣候變遷更凸顯了代際不正義。當前的決策往往由中老年人主導，卻是青年與未來世代要承擔最大的環境代價。極端氣候、資源枯竭、生態崩壞，這些危機不僅是環境問題，更是一種代際倫理挑戰。當青年呼喊「氣候正義」時，他們真正要求的是一種文明的責任：不要用當代的繁榮，換取後代的毀滅。這也是為什麼「OK Boomer」或「Fridays for Future」之類的語言與行動，成為全球青年最鮮明的世代抗議。

Beyond economics and housing, climate change exposes an even deeper layer of generational injustice. Today's decisions are led by older generations, but the heaviest costs will be borne by the young and those yet to come. Extreme weather, resource depletion, and ecological collapse are not just environmental crises but ethical ones between generations. When youth call for "climate justice," they are demanding civilizational responsibility: do not trade present prosperity for future destruction. This is why slogans like "OK Boomer" and movements like "Fridays for Future" have become powerful symbols of generational protest worldwide.

第五章：
世代不正義的病根

Chapter Five:
The Roots of Generational Injustice

第一節：透支未來的經濟模式
Section 1: Growth Models That Borrow from the Future

當代經濟長期以「增長」作為唯一指標，卻忽略了
這種增長往往來自於透支未來。政府以債務刺激需求，
企業以過度開發壓榨資源，社會則以提前消費填補幻象。
這種模式表面上創造了繁榮，實際上卻將
風險與代價轉嫁給下一代。
年輕人不僅要承擔公共債務的利息，
還要面對資源稀缺與環境惡化。當「明天的安全」
被用來換取「今天的繁榮」，
世代不正義就成為經濟結構的必然結果。

Modern economies have long treated “growth” as the sole metric of success, yet this growth is often achieved by borrowing from the future. Governments stimulate demand through debt, corporations exploit resources through overdevelopment, and societies sustain illusions with premature consumption. On the surface, this creates prosperity; in reality, it shifts risks and costs onto the next generation. Young people must shoulder both the interest on public debt and the consequences of resource depletion and environmental decline. When “tomorrow’s security” is traded for “today’s prosperity,” generational injustice becomes an inevitable outcome of economic design.

第二節：金融化與資產崇拜
Section 2: Financialization and the Cult of Assets

隨著資本市場的擴張，金融資產取代了實質勞動，成為社會分配的核心。房地產、股票、債券等資產價格不斷飆升，而薪資卻停滯不前。上一代因房地產升值而積累財富，年輕人則因高房價和租金而被排除在外。社會逐漸形成「資產階級」與「無產世代」的斷裂，勞動的尊嚴被壓縮，擁有資產與否成了決定命運的分水嶺。金融化不僅改變了分配邏輯，也把整個世代推向更深的不平等。

With the expansion of capital markets, financial assets have replaced labor as the core of social distribution. Real estate, stocks, and bonds soar in value while wages stagnate. Older generations accumulate wealth through property appreciation, while the young are excluded by high prices and rents. Society fractures into “asset-holders” and a “generation without assets,” as the dignity of labor is compressed and ownership becomes the decisive line of destiny. Financialization not only alters the logic of distribution but pushes entire generations into deeper inequality.

第三節：短視政治與老人綁架
Section 3: Short-Sighted Politics and the Grip of the Elderly

民主社會的政治人物往往追求短期選票利益，而忽視長期世代責任。老人因投票率高而成為政策討好的主要對象，年金、醫療補助不斷擴張，卻缺乏對年輕世代的支持。結果是「老人綁架」：政治為了維持穩定，犧牲了未來。這種短視不僅削弱了政策的前瞻性，也讓青年感受到被排除，覺得自己只是被迫承擔而無法決定的納稅機器。當代民主若無法解決這種結構性的傾斜，將逐漸失去年輕人的信任。

In democratic societies, politicians often chase short-term electoral gains while ignoring long-term intergenerational responsibility. With high voter turnout among the elderly, policies expand pensions and healthcare subsidies but neglect support for the young. The result is “elder capture”: politics sacrifices the future for present stability. This short-sightedness not only weakens policy foresight but also leaves youth feeling excluded, reduced to tax-paying machines burdened without choice. If contemporary democracies cannot address this structural skew, they risk losing the trust of younger generations.

第四節：資源掠奪與環境危機
Section 4: Resource Extraction and the Environmental Crisis

世代不正義不只存在於金錢分配，也存在於自然資源的掠奪。上一代以工業化與消費驅動成長，卻留下污染、氣候變遷與生態破壞。年輕人與未來世代必須承受極端氣候、糧食不穩與生態崩壞的後果，卻幾乎沒有參與決策的權利。當代文明透支的不只是財政與金融，更是地球本身的承載力。這種資源與環境上的不義，使得代際公平不再只是經濟問題，而是人類能否繼續延續的核心考驗。

Generational injustice is not confined to financial distribution but extends to the exploitation of natural resources. Older generations drove growth through industrialization and consumption, leaving behind pollution, climate change, and ecological damage. Young people and future generations must bear the consequences—extreme weather, food insecurity, and ecosystem collapse—without having had meaningful say in the decisions. Contemporary civilization has not only overdrawn its fiscal and financial accounts but also the carrying capacity of the planet. This injustice in resources and environment makes intergenerational equity not just an economic issue but a core test of human survival.

世代不正義的病根，並非單一政策的失誤，而是整個
文明運作邏輯的扭曲：以短視取代長遠，以資產取代勞動，
以掠奪取代永續。這些結構性的問題，讓年輕人即使努力，
也無法逃脫制度設計的陷阱。
要真正理解世代不正義，必須看清它的根源，
而不只是症狀。下一章，我們將討論可能的出路：
住房去金融化、基本收入、教育改革與新的世代契約，
如何能夠為被困的世代打開新的空間。

The roots of generational injustice lie not in isolated policy failures but in the distorted logic of civilization itself: short-termism over long-term vision, assets over labor, extraction over sustainability. These structural flaws trap young people in systems where effort cannot yield escape. To truly understand generational injustice, one must confront its roots rather than its symptoms. In the next chapter, we turn to possible pathways out: de-financialized housing, basic income, educational reform, and a new generational contract—ways to carve open space for a trapped generation.

第六章：解决之道

Chapter 6: Pathways to Solutions

第一節 住房去金融化
Section 1: De-Financializing Housing

要解決世代不正義，第一步就是讓「住房回歸居住本質」。
當房子被視為投資品時，青年永遠追不上資產膨脹的速度。
政府應推動囤房稅、空屋稅，限制投機炒作，並大規模興建
社會住宅，讓「居住權」回到公共政策的核心。
唯有讓年輕人能夠安居，社會才可能重建對未來的信任。

The first step to addressing generational injustice is restoring housing to its true purpose: shelter. When homes are treated as investment vehicles, young people can never keep pace with asset inflation. Governments must implement vacancy and hoarding taxes, curb speculation, and expand public housing to put the right to shelter back at the center of policy. Only when young people can secure a place to live can society begin to rebuild trust in the future.

第二節 基本收入與勞動新契約
Section 2: Basic Income and a New Labor Contract

長期的低薪與不穩定，就業市場已經讓青年失去規劃人生的自由。基本收入（UBI）或其他形式的生活保障，能為青年建立一個最低的安全網，使他們不必在生存與夢想之間二選一。同時，勞動制度必須從「壓榨」轉向「保障」，讓人類的價值不再由工時長短決定，而是由生活與創造力決定。

Persistent low wages and precarious work have stripped young people of the freedom to plan their lives. A Universal Basic Income (UBI), or similar forms of guaranteed living support, would provide a floor of security so that youth need not choose between survival and dreams. At the same time, labor systems must shift from exploitation to protection, valuing human life not by the hours worked but by the quality of life and creativity sustained.

第三節 年金改革與世代公平
Section 3: Pension Reform and Generational Fairness

年金制度若不改革，世代矛盾只會惡化。
政治不能再一味討好老人，而要建立世代平衡的制度：
減少對年輕人的稅收壓力，確保繳費與給付的公平，
並以消費型稅制（如增值稅）取代過度依賴所得稅。
如此一來，青年不再只是「繳稅機器」，
而能在公平的制度下展望自己的未來。

Without pension reform, generational conflict will only deepen. Politics can no longer cater exclusively to the elderly; it must create balanced systems: reducing the tax burden on the young, ensuring fairness between contributions and benefits, and shifting from overreliance on income tax toward consumption-based taxation (such as VAT). In this way, young people will no longer feel like “tax machines” but can instead envision their future under a fairer system.

第四節 教育去文憑化
Section 4: De-Credentializing Education

教育應該是開啟可能性的道路，而不是製造焦慮的工廠。要打破文憑至上的幻覺，社會必須承認技能、經驗與創造力的價值。政府應減少不必要的考試依賴，推動職業教育與終身學習，讓青年不再陷入「分數怪物」與「文憑蠢貨」的陷阱。教育應該是解放，而不是枷鎖。

Education should be a pathway to possibility, not a factory of anxiety. To break the illusion of credentialism, societies must recognize the value of skills, experience, and creativity. Governments should reduce overreliance on exams, promote vocational education and lifelong learning, and free youth from the traps of "score monsters" and "credential fools." Education must serve as liberation, not as a shackle.

第五節 世代永續契約
Section 5: A New Intergenerational Contract for Sustainability

世代不正義的根源，在於上一代透支了未來。因此，
必須重建一份新的「代際契約」：
老人不再守住特權，而是願意與青年共享資源；
青年不再被迫承擔過度責任，而能夠參與制度設計；
政府則有義務將氣候、財政與資源政策，
納入世代公平的框架。唯有如此，
社會才能恢復代際之間的信任，把未來還給未來的人。

The roots of generational injustice lie in the overdrawing of the future by older generations. Thus, a new "intergenerational contract" must be built: the elderly must relinquish privileges and share resources; the young must no longer be overburdened but empowered to shape institutions; governments must embed climate, fiscal, and resource policies within a framework of generational fairness. Only then can society restore trust between generations and return the future to those who truly live in it.

解決之道，不是靠單一方案，而是透過制度的全面調整。住房、收入、年金與教育改革，構成了一套「政策工具箱」，它們不是終點，而是打開未來的鑰匙。接下來，我們要回到更深層的反思：如果這些改革是必要的，那麼世代不正義究竟把整個文明推到了什麼樣的臨界點？這正是第七章「中場反思」要面對的問題。

The pathway forward is not a single fix but comprehensive systemic adjustment. Housing, income, pension, and education reforms form a "policy toolbox"—not endpoints but keys to unlocking the future. Next, we return to a deeper reflection: if these reforms are necessary, what kind of tipping point has generational injustice brought our civilization to? That is the question addressed in Chapter Seven, our "midway reflection."

第七章：
世代不正義的文明臨界點

Chapter Seven: The Civilizational Tipping Point of Generational Injustice

第一節：數據之外的真實
Section 1: The Reality Beyond the Numbers

世代不正義，常被簡化為經濟數據的比較：薪資停滯、房價所得比、失業率、年金缺口。然而，真正的危機遠不止於此。當青年長期生活在焦慮與壓迫中，他們的智力、情緒與創造力都會被削弱。研究顯示，當人不斷擔心賬單或生存時，智商平均下降十五點，這意味著社會集體智慧也在被拖累。換言之，數據只呈現冰山一角，真正的傷害是文明本身失去創造的引擎。

Generational injustice is often simplified into comparisons of economic data: stagnant wages, house price-to-income ratios, unemployment rates, pension deficits. Yet the real crisis extends beyond numbers. When youth live under constant anxiety and survival pressure, their intelligence, emotions, and creativity erode. Research shows that chronic financial stress can lower IQ by an average of fifteen points, meaning collective societal intelligence is also dragged down. In other words, data shows only the tip of the iceberg—the deeper damage is the loss of civilization's creative engine.

第二節：文明幻象的崩解
Section 2: The Collapse of Civilizational Illusions

每個時代都有其「幻象」：分數帶來公平競爭，文憑帶來穩定工作，資產帶來安全生活。然而，當這些幻象一一破滅，人們才發現自己只是被制度馴化的齒輪。青年被教育告訴要相信努力，卻在現實裡發現努力無法兌現；社會承諾「上升的梯子」，卻在制度裡拔掉了梯級。當幻象失效，文明便進入信任危機，世代之間的裂痕不再只是經濟差距，而是認知與價值的斷層。

Every era sustains its illusions: that test scores guarantee fairness, diplomas ensure stable jobs, and assets provide security. Yet when these illusions collapse, people discover they were merely cogs trained by institutions. Youth are told by education to believe in effort, only to find effort unrewarded in reality. Society promises “ladders of mobility,” while institutions quietly remove the rungs. Once illusions fail, civilization enters a crisis of trust, where the fracture between generations is not only economic but also cognitive and moral.

第三節：代際不正義的三重矛盾
Section 3: The Triple Contradictions of Generational Injustice

世代不正義是一種「三重矛盾」。第一，它是經濟的矛盾：青年努力卻無法改善生活，資源集中在老人與資產持有者。第二，它是文化的矛盾：長輩用過去的成功公式要求青年，卻無法理解環境已經改變。第三，它是倫理的矛盾：上一代用政策保障自己，卻把代價轉嫁給下一代。這三重矛盾交織，讓青年失去對制度的信任，也讓整個文明陷入自我消耗。

Generational injustice embodies a "triple contradiction." First, it is economic: youth labor yet fail to improve their lives, while resources concentrate with the elderly and asset-holders. Second, it is cultural: elders demand that youth follow outdated formulas of success, ignoring changed realities. Third, it is ethical: one generation protects itself through policy while shifting the costs onto the next. These three contradictions intertwine, eroding trust in institutions and pushing civilization into self-consumption.

第四節：臨界點的徵候
Section 4: Signs of a Civilizational Tipping Point

當世代不正義蔓延至社會的每一層面時，
它不僅是「青年困境」，而是「文明危機」。青年的退縮、
低生育率、腦力流失、社會信任崩塌，這些現象彼此疊加，
就像一條被拉到極限的繩索，隨時可能斷裂。
歷史上，文明的衰敗往往不是來自外敵，
而是來自內部信任與制度的耗竭。今天的世代不正義，
正是我們時代的警鐘，提醒我們已站在臨界點：
如果不改變，文明將難以為繼。

When generational injustice permeates every layer of society, it is no longer a "youth problem" but a "civilizational crisis." Youth withdrawal, low fertility, brain drain, and collapsing trust accumulate like strands of a rope stretched to its breaking point. Historically, civilizations often fell not from external enemies but from internal exhaustion of trust and institutions. Today's generational injustice is our era's alarm bell, signaling that we stand at the tipping point: without change, civilization itself may not endure.

本章不是要提出解方，而是要提醒：世代不正義是一面鏡子，
折射出整個文明的病灶。經濟的停滯、文化的誤解、
倫理的失衡，都在告訴我們，文明必須選擇新的方向。
這正是下半部的任務——不僅看見階級與世代如何交織，
還要探索跨世代、跨階級的合作，
並最終思考我們能否締造一份新的文明契約。

This chapter does not aim to provide solutions but to remind us: generational injustice is a mirror reflecting the illness of civilization. Economic stagnation, cultural misrecognition, and ethical imbalance all signal that civilization must choose a new direction. That is the task of the coming chapters—not only to examine how class and generation intertwine but also to explore alliances across them, and ultimately to ask whether we can forge a new civilizational contract.

第八章：
階級與世代的交織不平等

Chapter 8:
The Interwoven Inequalities of Class and Generation

第一節：資產繼承與起跑點不平等
Section 1: Inheritance and Unequal Starting Lines

在當代社會，青年之間的差距往往並非來自努力，
而是來自「出生時的起點」。若父母擁有房產、
股票或企業，子女便能輕易跨越同齡人無法達到的門檻。
相反，出身於無產家庭的青年，即便勤奮努力，
也常被高房價與債務壓得無法翻身。
階級的不平等透過資產繼承延續，
進一步與世代不正義交纏，讓「有資產的青年」
與「無資產的青年」
一開始就站在不同的軌道上。

In contemporary societies, the gap among youth is often less about effort and more about "the starting line of birth." Children of parents with property, stocks, or businesses easily leap barriers inaccessible to their peers. Conversely, those from assetless families, despite hard work, are weighed down by high housing costs and debt. Class inequality extends through inheritance and fuses with generational injustice, placing "asseted youth" and "assetless youth" on fundamentally different tracks from the outset.

第二節：教育如何再製階級
Section 2: How Education Reproduces Class

教育原本應該是改變命運的工具，但在現實中卻成為再製階級的機制。菁英家庭能投入更多資源在補習、國際學程與社會人脈，而弱勢家庭的孩子則被迫在應試教育中耗盡心力。即便進入大學，名校與非名校的差距依舊分化了未來的機會。於是，教育從「階級流動的梯子」逐漸變成「階級固化的圍牆」，青年在其中不是被解放，而是被篩選。

Education is supposed to be a tool for changing destiny, but in reality, it has become a mechanism of reproducing class. Elite families can invest more in tutoring, international programs, and social networks, while disadvantaged children exhaust themselves in exam-oriented schooling. Even in higher education, the divide between prestigious and non-prestigious universities continues to stratify opportunities. Thus, education shifts from being “a ladder of mobility” to “a wall of stratification,” where youth are not liberated but filtered.

第三節：青年世代的內部分裂
Section 3: The Internal Fracture Among Youth

當階級與世代交錯，青年本身也被分裂成不同群體。
有些青年因家族資產而能安心追求興趣，甚至投身創業；
另一些青年則因債務纏身而不得不在低薪與加班中掙扎。
這種「同代不同命」的現象，使青年難以形成共同的
世代意識。富二代與窮二代的落差，不僅是財富上的差距，
更是心理狀態與生活選擇的分歧，
進一步削弱了世代團結的可能性。

When class intersects with generation, youth themselves fracture into different groups. Some, backed by family assets, can confidently pursue passions or ventures; others, burdened by debt, are forced into cycles of low pay and overtime. This “same generation, different fates” phenomenon prevents youth from forming a cohesive generational identity. The divide between the children of the wealthy and those of the poor is not only about money but also about psychological states and life choices, further eroding the possibility of generational solidarity.

第四節：世代＋階級的惡性循環
Section 4: The Vicious Cycle of Class and Generation

階級不平等與世代不正義一旦交織，便形成惡性循環。資產豐厚的家庭能將資源轉化為下一代的優勢，進一步拉開差距；而無資產的家庭則世代累積困境，年輕人甚至在照顧父母的過程中更加窒息。這種雙重不公，讓社會不僅停滯，還逐漸撕裂成互不理解的群體。當青年內部已經被分化，世代對抗更容易被既得利益者操弄，使真正的改革變得更加困難。

Once class inequality and generational injustice intertwine, they form a vicious cycle. Families with assets convert resources into advantages for their children, widening the gap; families without assets accumulate hardship across generations, with youth suffocating further under parental care obligations. This dual injustice not only stalls society but fractures it into groups that cannot understand one another. When youth are internally divided, generational conflicts are more easily manipulated by vested interests, making genuine reform even harder to achieve.

階級與世代的不平等不是平行線，而是相互纏繞的鎖鏈。
它們使得不公義不僅橫向地分化青年，也縱向地固化世代。
要理解世代不正義，不能只看「青年與長輩的矛盾」，
還必須看見「青年內部的裂痕」。
下一章，我們將透過台灣、中國與全球的案例比較，
更清楚地看到這種交織如何在不同社會中具體展現，
並檢驗改革是否仍有突破的可能。

The inequalities of class and generation are not parallel lines but interlocking chains. They divide youth horizontally and entrench inequality vertically across generations. To grasp generational injustice fully, we must not only see the conflict between youth and elders but also the fractures within youth themselves. In the next chapter, we will compare cases from Taiwan, China, and the global context to see how these interwoven inequalities manifest concretely and to test whether reform remains possible.

第九章：案例比較——台灣、中國與全球的交織

Chapter Nine: Case Comparisons — Taiwan, China, and Global Intersections

第一節：低薪困境的不同樣貌
Section 1: Divergent Faces of Low Wages

台灣的22K世代，代表的是「薪資被凍結」的困境。青年進入職場，薪水長期停滯不前，生活成本卻不斷上升。中國則呈現另一種形式：青年投入漫長的學習與競爭，卻只能得到「高學歷、低報酬」的現實。相比之下，歐美千禧世代並非沒有成長的工資，而是被龐大的學貸與房貸抵消了所得。三者表面不同，但本質一致——「努力」與「報酬」已經脫節，青年不再能透過勤奮改善生活。

Taiwan's 22K generation represents wages that are effectively frozen. Youth enter the labor force with stagnant salaries even as living costs rise. In China, the form differs: years of study and fierce competition lead only to "high education, low pay." In contrast, Western millennials may see income growth but remain shackled by massive student debt and housing costs. While these expressions vary, their essence is the same—"effort" has decoupled from "reward," leaving young people unable to improve their lives through hard work.

第二節：住房金融化的共通壓力
Section 2: Housing Financialization as a Shared Burden

在台灣，房價高漲使青年無法安居，即使租屋也不穩定；中國的「六個錢包」模式，讓三代資產被一套房綁住，青年更背上沉重貸款；而在全球主要城市，青年成為「租不起的一代」，只能與室友合租或被迫遠距通勤。不同社會的解法各異——台灣靠政府補助，中國靠家庭支持，全球青年則延遲獨立——但共通的現象是，住房不再是「居住的權利」，而是「世代的枷鎖」。

In Taiwan, soaring prices block young people from stable housing, with renting itself insecure; in China, the “six wallets” model ties three generations’ wealth into a single property, while saddling youth with crushing mortgages; and in global cities, young people have become the “generation that can’t afford rent,” forced into shared flats or long commutes. The coping strategies differ—state subsidies in Taiwan, family pooling in China, delayed independence in the West—but the shared reality is that housing is no longer a “right to shelter” but a generational shackle.

第三節：家庭結構與代際責任的差異
Section 3: Family Structures and Varieties of Intergenerational Burden

台灣的青年雖然也需支持父母，但兄弟姊妹能分擔壓力；中國的獨生子女卻面對「421家庭結構」，一人照顧六位長輩，幾乎無法喘息；歐美青年則依賴國家社會保障體系，卻因人口老化而被課以更高稅負。三種模式看似不同，但核心是一樣的：制度缺口由青年填補，只是填補的方式不同——台灣以「家庭補貼＋低薪壓力」，中國以「單子女承擔」，歐美則以「高稅負＋福利壓縮」。

Taiwanese youth, though responsible for supporting parents, often share the duty with siblings. In China, only children face the "4-2-1 family structure," carrying six elders alone with little respite. In Europe and America, welfare states absorb eldercare, but demographic aging translates into heavier taxes on younger workers. These models look different, yet their essence is the same: young people fill systemic gaps, only by different means—through family subsidies and low pay in Taiwan, single-child burden in China, and high taxation with welfare squeeze in the West.

第四節：青年回應模式的比較
Section 4: Youth Responses in Comparative Perspective

台灣青年選擇沉默式抗議：不結婚、不生育、
人才外流，以「拒絕未來」來表達失望。
中國青年則以「躺平」作為消極抗爭，
拒絕投入無望的競爭。
歐美青年則更傾向於集體行動：
發起「氣候正義」「反學貸運動」等抗議，
要求制度改革。三種方式各異，
但都反映同一種情緒：當制度失去公信力，
青年就不再願意成為它的齒輪，
而是用沉默、退出或抗爭來表態。

Taiwanese youth practice silent protest: refusing marriage, delaying childbirth, or emigrating as a way of rejecting the future promised to them. Chinese youth embrace “lying flat” as passive resistance, withdrawing from futile competition. Western youth tend toward collective action: climate justice campaigns, student debt protests, and other movements demanding reform. These responses differ, yet all reflect the same sentiment: when institutions lose legitimacy, youth cease to be willing cogs, instead signaling their discontent through silence, withdrawal, or activism.

第五節：共通的結構性病灶
Section 5: Shared Structural Pathologies

比較台灣、中國與全球的案例，可以看到
三個共通的結構性病灶。
第一，資產與勞動的分配失衡：資產升值永遠快過薪資成長。
第二，政治的短視與迎合：政策不敢挑戰既得利益，
只能將負擔轉嫁給青年。
第三，責任的代際轉移：長輩保障自己，
卻要求青年承擔未來的不確定性。
這三重病灶，使不同社會都走上同一條道路——
把青年當成「最後的保險箱」，卻不給他們鑰匙。

Comparing Taiwan, China, and global cases reveals three shared structural pathologies. First, the imbalance between asset appreciation and wage growth, with assets always outpacing labor. Second, short-sighted, pandering politics that avoid challenging vested interests, shifting burdens onto youth instead. Third, the intergenerational transfer of responsibility, where elders secure their own protections while demanding youth shoulder future uncertainties. These pathologies place every society on the same trajectory—treating youth as the “final safety vault,” but denying them the keys.

台灣、中國與全球的世代不正義，表現各異卻
共通於結構性矛盾：勞動被貶值、資產被神化、
責任被轉嫁。不同的制度差異，只是讓青年以不同形式
承受同樣的重壓。
本章顯示，世代與階級的問題已不再能分開看待，
而必須放在同一張地圖上理解。
下一章，我們將嘗試描繪一份新的藍圖：跨世代與跨階
級的聯合方案，能否打破這張由不公義編織的網？

Generational injustice in Taiwan, China, and the world manifests differently but shares structural contradictions: labor devalued, assets glorified, and responsibilities shifted. Institutional differences only determine the form in which youth bear the same heavy burden. This chapter shows that class and generation can no longer be analyzed apart but must be mapped together. In the next chapter, we attempt to sketch a new blueprint: can a cross-generational and cross-class alliance break the web of injustice?

第十章：走向新契約——跨世代與跨階級的聯合方案

Chapter 10: Toward a New Contract — A Cross-Generational and Cross-Class Alliance

世代不正義與階級不平等交織在一起，
使得問題不再只是「青年對老人」，
或「窮人對富人」，
而是整個社會契約的斷裂。
單一的改革已不足以修復裂痕，
必須同時處理世代與階級的雙重不公。
這意味著，青年與老人、富者與窮者，
必須在新的框架下尋找共存之道：
一方面確保資源不再被少數家族壟斷，
另一方面也要讓每一代人都能在公平的制度中擁有未來。
這是一場新的文明契約，要求跨世代與跨階級的聯合，
否則社會將在分裂中走向衰敗。

The intertwining of generational injustice and class inequality means the problem is no longer merely "youth versus elders" or "poor versus rich," but the collapse of the social contract itself. Piecemeal reforms are no longer sufficient; both generational and class inequities must be addressed together. This requires youth and elders, the wealthy and the poor, to seek coexistence within a new framework: one that prevents resources from being monopolized by a few families while ensuring that every generation has a fair stake in the future. This is the foundation of a new civilizational contract, one that demands a cross-generational and cross-class alliance—without which society risks decline through division.

第一節 財富再分配機制
Section 1: Mechanisms for Wealth Redistribution

要打破世代與階級的雙重不平等，首要之務是
透過財富再分配。除了改革年金之外，
還必須強化遺產稅、資產稅與土地稅，
防止巨額財富透過繼承不斷集中在少數家族手中。
當資源被合理分配，社會才可能避免
「富二代壟斷未來」的惡性循環，
讓更多青年有機會透過自身努力獲得公平的起點。

To break the double bind of generational and class inequality, the first priority is wealth redistribution. Beyond pension reform, inheritance taxes, wealth taxes, and land value taxes must be strengthened to prevent massive fortunes from being perpetually concentrated within a few families. Only when resources are fairly distributed can society escape the vicious cycle of "second-generation elites monopolizing the future," and allow more young people a fairer chance to succeed through their own efforts.

第二節 重建社會流動性
Section 2: Rebuilding Social Mobility

教育不應只是文憑的比賽，而應是社會流動的橋樑。
要避免教育淪為階級再製的工具，
政府應降低補習與高等教育的門檻，
並提供跨階層的學習資源，例如公共獎助學金、
免費職業訓練、跨國交流計畫。
唯有讓來自不同階層的青年都能公平參與，
教育才能真正恢復「改變命運」的功能。

Education should not be a contest of credentials but a bridge for social mobility. To prevent education from becoming a tool of class reproduction, governments must lower the barriers to tutoring and higher education, while providing cross-class opportunities such as public scholarships, free vocational training, and international exchange programs. Only when youth from all backgrounds have equal access can education truly reclaim its role as a pathway to changing one's destiny.

第三節 普惠資源制度
Section 3: Universal Resource Sharing Systems

除了基本收入，社會還需要建立「全民共享紅利」的制度。
例如，碳稅返還可以將氣候政策的成本轉化為全民紅利；
自然資源收益基金可以將土地與能源的收入分配給所有公民。
這種普惠制度能夠同時減少階級差距，
也緩解代際矛盾，因為每一代人
都能分享社會與自然資源的成果。

Beyond basic income, societies need systems of universal resource sharing. For example, carbon tax dividends can transform the costs of climate policies into public benefits, and sovereign wealth funds based on land and energy revenues can distribute returns to all citizens. Such universal mechanisms reduce class disparities while easing generational tensions, ensuring that every generation shares in the fruits of social and natural resources.

第四節 跨世代與跨階級的政治聯合
Section 4: Cross-Generational and Cross-Class Political Alliances

要推動改革，
青年不能只把焦點放在「反對老人」，
窮人也不能只與「富人對抗」。
真正的力量來自跨世代與跨階級的政治聯合：
青年與長者一同要求年金公平，工薪族與小資產階層
共同支持住房去金融化。唯有這樣的聯合，
才能避免被既得利益者分化，
形成足以推動制度變革的集體力量。

Reform requires more than youth opposing elders or the poor opposing the rich. Real power lies in cross-generational and cross-class political alliances: young and old demanding pension fairness together, wage earners and small asset-holders supporting de-financialization of housing. Only through such alliances can society avoid being divided by vested interests and build the collective strength needed to drive institutional change.

第五節 共享未來的文明契約
Section 5: A Civilizational Contract for a Shared Future

世代與階級的雙重不平等，最終是一場文明危機。
解方不僅是技術性的制度改革，更是一份新的倫理承諾：
上一代願意放下特權，富裕階層願意分享資源，
青年願意承擔責任，弱勢群體得到保障。
這是一份「共享未來」的文明契約，
它要求我們不再把希望建立在掠奪，
而是建立在合作。唯有如此，
人類才能走出分裂與對立，迎向共同的繁榮。

The double inequality of generation and class is ultimately a civilizational crisis. The solution is not only technical reforms but also a new ethical commitment: older generations must relinquish privileges, the wealthy must share resources, youth must shoulder responsibility, and the vulnerable must be protected. This is a civilizational contract for a “shared future,” one built not on exploitation but on cooperation. Only then can humanity move beyond division and conflict toward shared prosperity.

世代不正義與階級不平等並非孤立的問題，
而是相互交織的結構性病灶。解決之道也不能
停留在單一政策或短期方案，而必須同時從制度設計、
財富分配、教育公平與代際倫理等層面，
重建一個能長期維持社會信任的框架。
這樣的框架不會立刻消除所有矛盾，
但能逐步修補代際與階級的裂痕，
使社會重新具備向前推進的基礎。

Generational injustice and class inequality are not isolated issues but intertwined structural pathologies. Solutions cannot rest on single policies or short-term fixes; they must rebuild a framework that integrates institutional design, wealth redistribution, educational equity, and intergenerational ethics to restore long-term social trust. Such a framework will not instantly erase all conflicts, but it can gradually mend the fractures of generation and class, providing society with the foundations it needs to move forward.

第十一章：
親身見證

Chapter 11:
Personal Testimonies

第一節：重返校園的驚愕
Section 1: Returning to Campus in Midlife

四十二歲那年，我再次踏入大學校園，
與二十歲出頭的青年同學並肩而坐。起初，我以為自己只是來完成知識的延伸，卻意外看見一代人的焦慮。
課堂上，教授侃侃而談，但下課後，學生們的對話卻不再是夢想或理想，而是「打工時數」「房租壓力」「學貸還款」。我才真正感受到，制度的重擔如何
壓在這些年輕人身上，
他們的青春不再是探索的旅程，而是生存的賭局。

At the age of forty-two, I stepped once more into a university campus, sitting shoulder to shoulder with students barely in their twenties. I thought I was simply extending my learning, but instead I witnessed a generation's anxiety. In class, professors lectured with ease, but after class, conversations revolved not around dreams or ideals, but "work hours," "rent stress," and "loan repayments." It was then I realized how heavily the system's burdens weigh upon them. Their youth is no longer a journey of exploration but a gamble for survival.

第二節：台灣與美國的兩次大學對比
Section 2: Contrasting My Two College Experiences in Taiwan and the U.S.

回想我自己的大學歲月，曾經是充滿自由與選擇的年代。在台灣，我的求學幾乎沒有太大的經濟壓力；而在美國，作為單身的亞洲女性與綠卡持有者，我得到全額 Pell Grant，再加上音樂系提供的獎學金，幾乎讓我的學費全免。更幸運的是，因為所有便宜宿舍早已額滿，只剩下最昂貴的雙人學生公寓，而我能靠獎助學金承擔這筆費用，反而住進條件最佳的宿舍。

Looking back at my own college years, they were a time filled with freedom and choice. In Taiwan, my studies carried little financial burden; in the United States, as a single Asian woman with a green card, I was awarded a full Pell Grant along with scholarships from the music department, which nearly eliminated my tuition costs. By sheer luck, all the cheaper dormitories were already filled, leaving only the most expensive two-person student apartment, and thanks to my grants I could afford it—ironically placing me in the best housing option.

我擁有獨立浴室，只需與室友共用廚房與客廳，
這使我未經歷過今日青年常見的
「多人共租、共用衛浴」處境。
這樣的條件，讓我能安心學習與練琴，
不必背負沉重的生存焦慮；但對於當代青年而言，
即便進入同樣的大學，他們卻往往要背負龐大的學貸，
並被迫與多人合租、打工維生。
這種強烈的落差，讓我深刻體會到：同樣的教育制度，
在不同世代，竟能承載如此懸殊的重量。

I had my own private bathroom and shared only the kitchen and living room with a roommate, which meant I never experienced the cramped reality of shared bathrooms and overcrowded rentals that so many young people endure today. These conditions allowed me to focus on study and piano practice without the crushing anxiety of survival; but for today's students, even at the same universities, the experience is radically different—burdened with debt, forced into shared housing, and juggling jobs. The contrast made me realize how the same educational system can impose vastly different weights across generations.

第三節：財務壓力下的學習斷裂
Section 3: Learning Under the Weight of Financial Pressure

研究顯示，當人長期處於財務憂慮時，智商平均會下降十五點。當我看著同學一邊打哈欠、一邊趕報告時，這項數據在眼前活了起來。他們不是不聰明，而是被焦慮吞噬。帳單、貸款、未來的不確定，使他們的專注力與創造力被不斷消耗。學習應該是心智最自由的時刻，卻被迫成為焦慮的牢籠。這種對青年潛能的浪費，正是世代不正義最隱蔽卻最致命的後果。

Studies show that chronic financial stress can lower IQ by an average of fifteen points. Watching my classmates yawn through lectures while rushing to finish assignments, I saw this statistic come alive. They were not lacking intelligence—they were being devoured by anxiety. Bills, debt, and uncertain futures drained their focus and creativity. Learning should be a time of mental freedom, yet it has become a cage of anxiety. This squandering of youth potential is one of generational injustice's most hidden yet most lethal consequences.

第四節：青年的心聲與沉默
Section 4: The Voices and Silences of Youth

課堂上，少數同學勇敢談到他們的憂慮：
有人說自己畢業後不敢回鄉，
因為薪水不足以支撐家庭；有人說打算延後結婚，
因為沒有房子；更多人則保持沉默，把壓力埋藏在心底。
這些沉默不是冷漠，而是一種無力感。
當制度不再值得信任，
年輕人學會的不是抗爭，而是「如何在夾縫中苟活」。
這種沉默比抗議更令人心碎，
因為它象徵希望正在被慢慢熄滅。

In class, a few students dared to voice their worries: one said he couldn't return home after graduation because wages couldn't support his family; another planned to delay marriage for lack of housing; most, however, remained silent, burying stress inside. Their silence was not indifference but helplessness. When systems no longer merit trust, young people do not learn to resist but to "survive in the cracks." Such silence is more heartbreaking than protest, for it signals hope being quietly extinguished.

第五節：跨世代的啟示
Section 5: Lessons Across Generations

透過這段親身經歷，我理解到世代不正義不是遙遠的理論，
而是活生生的現實。青年承受的焦慮、
被壓縮的選擇與消失的夢想，都是制度崩壞的證據。
而對我這樣中年的旁觀者而言，最大的啟示是：
改革不再是「為青年發聲」，
而是「為整個文明存續發聲」。
因為若一代人被迫放棄希望，
那麼下一代將連選擇希望的機會都失去。

Through this personal journey, I realized generational injustice is not an abstract theory but a lived reality. Youth anxiety, compressed choices, and vanished dreams are evidence of systemic collapse. For me, as a middle-aged witness, the greatest lesson is this: reform is no longer about "speaking for the young," but about "speaking for civilization's survival." For if one generation is forced to give up hope, the next will lose even the chance to choose it.

親身見證讓我們從數據回到真實，從制度回到生命。
青年不是冰冷統計的一部分，而是有血有肉的生命，
他們的焦慮與沉默正在塑造整個社會的未來。
下一章，我們將把視野拉高，
思考如何把世代與階級的聯合，
轉化為具體的行動與契約，
走向「新文明契約」的可能。

Personal testimonies bring us back from numbers to reality, from systems to lives. Youth are not part of cold statistics but living beings whose anxieties and silences shape society's future. In the next chapter, we broaden the perspective to ask: how can alliances across generations and classes be transformed into concrete actions and contracts, moving us toward the possibility of a "new civilizational pact"?

第十二章：
重建希望的文明契約

Chapter Twelve: Rebuilding a Civilizational Contract of Hope

第一節：世代不正義作為文明的警鐘
Section 1: Generational Injustice as a Civilizational Alarm

世代不正義不是一個孤立的社會議題，
而是一場文明的自我檢驗。當一代人努力
卻無法獲得應有的回報，當教育變成焦慮的陷阱，
當住房、勞動與年金制度都把未來壓在青年肩上，
這不僅是政策的失靈，更是文明運行邏輯的崩壞。
這種不正義就是一個警鐘，提醒我們：
如果我們選擇維持現狀，
那麼我們不僅犧牲的是一代人，
而是整個文明延續的可能。

Generational injustice is not an isolated social issue but a test of civilization itself. When one generation labors without fair reward, when education becomes a trap of anxiety, when housing, labor, and pensions all shift burdens onto youth, it is not merely a failure of policy but a breakdown of civilization's operating logic. This injustice is an alarm, warning us that if we choose to preserve the status quo, what we sacrifice is not only a generation but the very possibility of civilization's continuity.

第二節：留下未來的空間
Section 2: Preserving Space for the Future

真正的責任，不是滿足當下的利益，而是為未來留下生存與發展的空間。這意味著不能再透支資源、不能再掠奪環境、不能再讓青年為前人的錯誤買單。一個健康的文明，不是由財富的數字定義，而是由它能否保護下一代自由探索的可能來衡量。留下未來的空間，等於是承認：我們這一代不是文明的終點，而只是接力棒的暫時持有者。

True responsibility is not about satisfying present interests but about preserving room for future survival and growth. This means no longer overdrawing resources, no longer plundering the environment, no longer forcing youth to pay for the mistakes of their predecessors. A healthy civilization is not defined by wealth metrics but by its ability to protect the next generation's freedom to explore. To preserve space for the future is to acknowledge that our generation is not the endpoint of civilization but merely the temporary holder of its relay baton.

第三節：後代的責任與我們的選擇
Section 3: Responsibility to Descendants and Our Choices

文明的價值，不僅在於它能給予現代人什麼，更在於它是否願意承擔對後代的責任。如果我們把資產化、短視政治與環境掠奪視為理所當然，那麼我們給後代留下的不是遺產，而是負債。反之，如果我們選擇重新設計制度，建立普惠資源、跨世代公平與共享未來的契約，那麼我們交付給後代的將是一份希望。選擇在我們手裡，而後果卻將由後代承受。

The value of a civilization lies not only in what it provides to the present but in whether it assumes responsibility for the future. If we normalize financialization, short-term politics, and environmental exploitation, what we leave behind is not a legacy but a liability. Conversely, if we choose to redesign institutions to create universal resources, intergenerational fairness, and a shared future, what we deliver to our descendants will be hope. The choice is ours to make, but the consequences will be theirs to bear.

第四節：新文明契約的願景
Section 4: The Vision of a New Civilizational Contract

所謂「新文明契約」，不是一份抽象的宣言，
而是一份具體的行動指南：以世代永續為核心，讓財富不再壟斷於少數，讓教育不再淪為文憑陷阱，讓住房回到居住本質，讓基本收入保障尊嚴，讓環境政策為後代
留下一片可呼吸的天空。
這是一份超越世代與階級對立的契約，
它要求我們不再彼此爭奪，而是共同守護未來。

The so-called "new civilizational contract" is not an abstract manifesto but a concrete guide for action: placing generational sustainability at its core, ensuring wealth is not monopolized by the few, restoring education to its true purpose beyond diplomas, reclaiming housing as shelter, securing dignity through basic income, and leaving behind a breathable sky through environmental policy. This is a contract that transcends generational and class divides, calling us not to fight one another but to safeguard the future together.

第五節：希望作為公共財
Section 5: Hope as a Public Good

希望不能是少數人的奢侈品，
而必須是所有人的基本權利。
當青年能夠懷抱希望，社會才會有創造力；
當後代能夠擁有希望，文明才會有延續性。
這本書的最終呼籲，就是要把希望從市場的商品
與政治的籌碼，重新還原成一種公共財。
唯有如此，世代不正義才有被修復的可能，
而我們的文明才能真正邁向永續。

Hope cannot remain a luxury for the few but must become a basic right for all. When youth are able to hold on to hope, society has creativity; when descendants inherit hope, civilization has continuity. The final call of this book is to restore hope from being a market commodity or political bargaining chip into a public good. Only then can generational injustice be repaired, and only then can our civilization truly move toward sustainability.

作者簡介
Author Biography

徐萍，作家、鋼琴家、口譯員與社會制度改革倡議者。
多年來，她以雙語寫作，出版涵蓋教育、住房、稅制、
長照與基本收入等多領域的著作，致力於探索制度
如何影響人類的生活與未來。
42 歲時，她在美國重返大學校園，親身體驗跨世代的差異
與不平等，這段經歷也成為她書寫世代不正義的重要基礎。
她的作品結合理論分析與個人見證，既批判制度的不公，
也傳達對下一代的深切憐惜與關懷。

Ping Xu is a writer, pianist, interpreter, and advocate for social system reform. Over the years, she has written bilingually and published extensively on education, housing, taxation, long-term care, and basic income, exploring how institutions shape human lives and futures. At the age of 42, she returned to university in the United States, personally experiencing the disparities and inequalities between generations—an experience that deeply informs her work on generational injustice. Blending structural analysis with personal testimony, her writings critique systemic unfairness while conveying a profound compassion and concern for the younger generation.

www.ingramcontent.com/pod-product-compliance
Lightning Source LLC
LaVergne TN
LVHW090331210926
848480LV00004B/1377

9798349558771